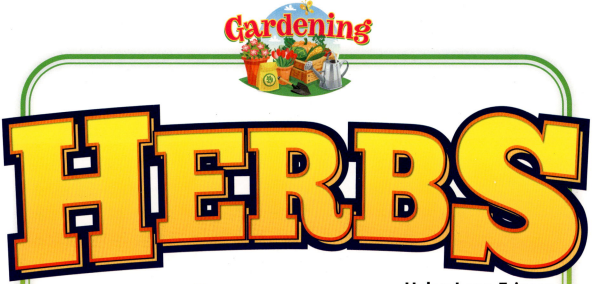

HERBS

Helen Lepp Friesen

www.av2books.com

Step 1
Go to **www.av2books.com**

Step 2
Enter this unique code

OBKWMABHW

Step 3
Explore your interactive eBook!

CONTENTS
- 4 All about Herbs
- 6 Why Plant an Herb Garden?
- 8 The Life Cycle of an Herbaceous Plant
- 10 When to Plant
- 12 Where to Plant
- 14 Herb Gardens in the United States
- 16 Choosing Your Herbs
- 18 Ready to Plant
- 20 Herb Garden Care
- 22 10-Question Herb Quiz

AV2 is optimized for use on any device

Your interactive eBook comes with...

Contents
Browse a live contents page to easily navigate through resources

Audio
Listen to sections of the book read aloud

Videos
Watch informative video clips

Weblinks
Gain additional information for research

Try This!
Complete activities and hands-on experiments

Key Words
Study vocabulary, and complete a matching word activity

Quizzes
Test your knowledge

Slideshows
View images and captions

This title is part of our AV2 digital subscription

1-Year K–5 Subscription
ISBN 978-1-7911-3320-7

Access hundreds of AV2 titles with our digital subscription.
Sign up for a FREE trial at **www.av2books.com/trial**

HERBS

CONTENTS

AV2 Book Code	2
All about Herbs	4
Why Plant an Herb Garden?	6
The Life Cycle of an Herbaceous Plant	8
When to Plant	10
Where to Plant	12
Herb Gardens in the United States	14
Choosing Your Herbs	16
Ready to Plant	18
Herb Garden Care	20
10-Question Herb Quiz	22
Key Words/Index	23

All about Herbs

If you were to grow an herb garden, what types of herbs would you plant? Why did you choose these ones? Do they taste good? Do you like how they look or smell?

Planting a garden can help you learn about the herbs that grow best in your region. You will find out what your herbs need to grow and be healthy. You can take care of them every day. Doing this brings many rewards. Fresh herbs are healthy and delicious!

> Many parts of a plant can be used to season food, but only the leaves are called herbs. Seasonings that come from the roots, stem, bark, seeds, or fruit of a plant are called spices.

What Is an Herb?

Herbs are the leaves of plants that are used to flavor food. **Herbaceous plants** have several parts.

Seeds
Seeds form inside flowers. New plants grow from seeds.

Flowers
Flowers are the colorful parts of the plant that grow at the end of the stem.

Leaves
Leaves are the green parts of the plant that grow from the stem.

Stem
The stem comes out of the soil. It is attached to the plant's roots.

Roots
Roots are the part of the plant that is underground.

The **best-selling** herb in the United States is **basil**.

There are about **75** to **100** different kinds of herbs grown worldwide.

Why Plant an Herb Garden?

Herbs add pops of bright green to your windowsill or garden. Some herbs have a nice **fragrance**. These plants are important for other reasons as well.

People grow herbs to use in cooking. Planting your own herbs can save money. You will always have fresh herbs on hand to add flavor and color to dishes. You can even dry your herbs to use later. Recipes often require smaller amounts of dried herbs because they have a stronger flavor than fresh herbs.

Some herbs can be used as medicine. Peppermint is often made into a tea to help soothe an upset stomach.

Parsley makes a nice **garnish** on a meal.

Dill can be used to make pickles.

The Life Cycle of an Herbaceous Plant

All herbaceous plants begin life, grow, and make more plants. This is the life cycle of an herbaceous plant.

Seed
Herbaceous plants begin life as seeds. A seed will grow once it is planted.

Pollination
Insects and other animals carry **pollen** from one flower to another. New seeds are made. The cycle begins again.

Roots
When the seed grows, it produces roots. The roots hold the plant in the soil.

Seedling
A stem sprouts up out of the ground and starts to grow leaves. This small plant is called a seedling.

Flowers
Flowers grow from the stem of the plant.

When to Plant

What is the weather like where you live? Is it very hot in the summer? Do you have long winters? Herbs need certain conditions to grow well.

If you are going to plant herbs outside, you need to plant them at the right time of year. If it is too cold, they may not grow. Most people plant herbs in the spring. Herbs that do well in the spring are lemon balm and basil. Herbs that enjoy the summer sunshine are dill and mint.

Cilantro thrives in the spring. It can be eaten fresh or cooked.

SUMMER

Oregano loves the summer heat. It is often used in pizza sauce.

FALL

Planting herbs in the fall lets their roots grow big enough to last through the winter until spring.

At up to **$5,000 per pound**, saffron is the **most expensive** spice in the world.

Finely chopping fresh herbs releases **more oils**, which makes the herbs **taste better**.

Where to Plant

It is important that you choose the right place to plant your herbs. How do you know if a place is right? There are three main factors you should consider.

Light

Your herb garden should be somewhere with plenty of light. If you plant outside, your herbs can get their light from the Sun. If you plant inside, your herbs should be near a window.

Water

Water is necessary for herbs to survive. Some herbs need more water than others. Plant outdoor herbs where rainwater can reach them. If you are planting indoors, use a watering can to water your herbs.

Nutrients

Herbs need **nutrients** to grow. Try to choose soil that is enriched with nutrients. Another option is to add nutrients to the soil yourself, by using **compost**.

Herb Gardens in the United States

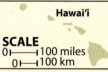

LEGEND
- California
- Washington
- Ohio
- Washington, D.C.
- Other Land

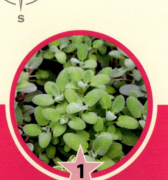

1. Pearson's Gardens & Herb Farm
Vista, California

Pearson's grows the biggest selection of herbs and spices in California. Almost 2,500 kinds of plants are produced here.

2. Trout Lake Farm
Trout Lake, Washington

Trout Lake Farm is the largest organic medicinal herb farm in the country. It produces more than 2.6 million pounds (1.2 million kilograms) of herbs every year.

There are many herb gardens in the United States. Some are inside, while others are outside. Herbs can be found in **arboretums** or **botanical** gardens. Some of these places are open to the public. People are welcome to visit and enjoy the fragrance of the herbs.

3
Cleveland Botanical Garden
Cleveland, Ohio

This botanical garden has one of the country's most significant herb gardens. About 3,500 plants grow in its nine themed sections.

4
The National Herb Garden (NHG)
Washington, D.C.

Located at the U.S. National Arboretum, the NHG was first constructed in 1980. Today, it is the largest designed herb garden in the country.

Choosing Your Herbs

There are so many herbs in the world. How do you decide which ones to grow in your herb garden? Will your herbs be outside or inside? If you are planting outside, research which herbs grow best in the **climate** where you live. If you are planting inside, you may need to get a **grow light** for your herbs. Also consider how much time you want to invest. Caring for some kinds of herbs takes more time than others.

One reason basil is such a popular herb choice is because it can be grown almost anywhere. It does well outdoors in a garden or indoors in a pot.

Annuals

Annuals need to be planted each year. They last for one growing season only. You can **harvest** their seeds at the end of the season and plant them the next year.

Summer Savory

Chervil

Cilantro

Chives

Perennials

Perennials only need to be planted once. After that, they grow every year. These herbs are easier to maintain than annuals.

Sage

Lavender

Ready to Plant

If you want to grow a successful garden, you have to start with the right equipment. You also have to follow the planting process.

Gardening Equipment

Trowel

A trowel is a small, handheld shovel. With it, you can make holes in the soil to plant herb seeds or seedlings.

Labels

It is a good idea to label your plants. That way, you will remember which herbs you planted and where they are.

Watering Can

Using a watering can allows you to sprinkle water over particular herbs, while keeping others dry.

The Planting Process

1. Use your trowel to loosen the soil.

2. Dig a small hole for the herb seed or seedling. Be sure to check the recommended planting depth, as this varies from herb to herb.

3. Place the seed or seedling in the hole.

4. Put the soil back in the hole and gently push it down with your hands. If planting a seedling, push the soil around the plant.

5. Use your watering can to soak the soil around the seed or seedling.

Repeat for each seed or seedling you plant.

Herb Garden Care

Taking care of an herb garden does not stop with planting. You must check on it every day to make sure that the plants are growing and staying healthy. There are three main areas that could need attention.

Watering

Check the soil in your herb garden to see if it needs water. Most herbs require water about once per week, when the soil feels dry to the touch.

Weeds

Weeds take up the space, nutrients, and water your herbs need to grow. Make sure to remove any weeds that you see. Pull them with your hands or dig them out with a trowel.

Harvest

Herbs taste best if picked before they **bloom**. It is best to harvest your herbs regularly to help encourage new growth. Continue harvesting for the rest of the season.

10 Question Herb Quiz

1 Which herb can be used to make pickles?

2 What is the best-selling herb in the United States?

3 Herbs are which part of a plant?

4 What carries pollen from one flower to another?

5 Which farm has the biggest selection of herbs and spices in California?

6 What are three factors to consider for your herbs to grow and stay healthy?

7 What are three examples of perennial herbs?

8 Why is it a good idea to label your herbs?

9 When is the best time to harvest your herbs?

10 Why must you weed your herb garden?

ANSWERS 1. Dill **2.** Basil **3.** The leaves **4.** Insects and other animals **5.** Pearson's Gardens & Herb Farm **6.** Light, water, and nutrients **7.** Chives, sage, and lavender **8.** So you will remember which herbs you planted and where they are **9.** Before they bloom **10.** Because weeds take up the space, nutrients, and water your herbs need to grow.

Key Words

arboretums: places where trees, shrubs, and other plants are grown for scientific and educational purposes

bloom: when a mature flower produces a colorful head to attract pollinators

botanical: relating to plants

climate: the weather in a particular place over a period of time

compost: decaying plant material used for nutrients in the soil

fragrance: a pleasant, sweet smell

garnish: a decoration that adds color or flavor to a plate of food

grow light: a lamp used for growing plants indoors that emits light similar to that of the Sun

harvest: to pick or collect

herbaceous plants: soft plants with little or no woody tissue

nutrients: substances that promote growth

pollen: a dust made by plants that helps them develop seeds

Index

annuals 17

Cleveland Botanical Garden 15
climate 16
color 5, 6

equipment 18

flowers 5, 8, 9, 22

insects 8, 22

labels 18, 22
leaves 4, 5, 9, 22

National Herb Garden, The 15
nutrients 13, 21, 22

Pearson's Gardens & Herb Farm 14, 22
perennials 17, 22
pollen 8, 22

roots 4, 5, 9, 11

seedling 9, 18, 19
seeds 4, 5, 8, 9, 17, 18, 19
shovel 18
soil 5, 9, 13, 18, 19, 20
stem 4, 5, 9
Sun 10, 12

Trout Lake Farm 14
trowel 18, 19, 21

water 13, 18, 20, 21, 22
watering can 13, 18, 19
weeds 21, 22

Get the best of both worlds.

AV2 bridges the gap between print and digital.

The expandable resources toolbar enables quick access to content including **videos**, **audio**, **activities**, **weblinks**, **slideshows**, **quizzes**, and **key words**.

Animated videos make static images come alive.

Resource icons on each page help readers to further **explore key concepts**.

Published by AV2
276 5th Avenue
Suite 704 #917
New York, NY 10001
Website: www.av2books.com

Copyright ©2022 AV2
All rights reserved. No part of this publication may be reproduced, stored in a retrieval system, or transmitted in any form or by any means, electronic, mechanical, photocopying, recording, or otherwise, without the prior written permission of the publisher.

Library of Congress Cataloging-in-Publication Data
Names: Friesen, Helen Lepp, 1961- author.
Title: Herbs / Helen Lepp Friesen.
Description: New York, NY : AV2, [2022] | Series: Gardening | Includes index. | Audience: Grades 2-3
Identifiers: LCCN 2020022327 (print) | LCCN 2020022328 (ebook) | ISBN 9781791127756 (library binding) | ISBN 9781791127763 (paperback) | ISBN 9781791127770 (ebook other) | ISBN 9781791127787 (ebook other)
Subjects: LCSH: Herbs--Juvenile literature.
Classification: LCC SB351.H5 F75 2021 (print) | LCC SB351.H5 (ebook) | DDC 615.3/21--dc23
LC record available at https://lccn.loc.gov/2020022327
LC ebook record available at https://lccn.loc.gov/2020022328

Printed in Guangzhou, China
1 2 3 4 5 6 7 8 9 0 25 24 23 22 21

022021
101120

Editor: Katie Gillespie
Art Director: Terry Paulhus

Every reasonable effort has been made to trace ownership and to obtain permission to reprint copyright material. The publisher would be pleased to have any errors or omissions brought to its attention so that they may be corrected in subsequent printings. AV2 acknowledges Getty Images, Newscom, iStock, and Shutterstock as its primary image suppliers for this title.

View new titles and product videos at www.av2books.com